WEST COUNTRY COOKING

Baking

Michael Raffael

Supported by Objective
5b EAGGF Funds

HALSGROVE

Foreword

Some of the West Country's baking specialities, pasties or Bath Buns, enjoy a national reputation. Others, saffron bread in Cornwall or Wiltshire Lardy Cake have a strong local following. Apart from these ever popular recipes, other cakes, pies and biscuits remain the secret of a handful of dedicated cooks or teeter on the verge of extinction.

Many in this category, a kind of endangered culinary species, deserve a better fate. The Devizes Cheesecake in its original form is every bit as good as a Bakewell Pudding. St Catherine's Cake has a unique shape and texture. Clifton Puffs outstrip Banbury Cakes to which they are closely related.

The region does indeed have a rich heritage. In this book I have tried to pull together its many strands, the popular, the strange, the curious and the modern as a tribute to the home cooks, chefs and bakers who created it.

RECIPE PAGE 24/36

RECIPE PAGE 35

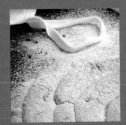

RECIPE PAGE 59

RECIPE PAGE 13

RECIPE PAGE 43

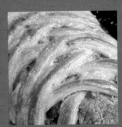

RECIPE PAGE 63

RECIPE PAGE 23

RECIPE PAGE 49

RECIPE PAGE 67

RECIPE PAGE 53

Contents

Cornwall

Cornish Cloam ovens are simply holes in chimney walls, oval-shaped and roofed over with a clay finish which gives them their name.

'Blackthorn was the favourite fuel for heating it with, and the ashes had to be kept raked out, so the bottom would get hot as well as the sides and roof. When it was white 'ot to the very door, the ashes were thoroughly cleaned out and the tins of bread and plum cake put in (our oven would hold ten tins), the door was shut and red ashes piled around it to keep out any draught, and there was nothing to do till it was ready to come out an hour later, a lot less trouble and a whole lot cleaner than black leading a new-fashioned apparatus to my mind.'

From St Kea W.I., published in *Cornish Recipes* 1929

Pasty

You never hear Cornishmen speak of 'Cornish pasty'. It's pasty pure and simple, to distinguish it from pork, vegetable, herby, kidney, liver and onion, date and windy pasties, variations on the original theme. Pasties are always a meal in themselves. Also, the meat and vegetables, go in raw. They're actually steamed inside their pastry shells.

Ann Muller of the Pasty shop on the Lizard and her mother, Hettie Merrick (author of *The Pasty Book*, Tor Mark 1995) the experts, say that pasties may not have originated in the Duchy, because they were eaten all over Britain two centuries ago, but they are properly linked to tin miners. The texture of the pastry has to be robust enough to withstand a bit of knocking and the tradition of marking each pasty with its owner's initials is less than 200 years old, not much when one considers that they have been around since Chaucer's time.

Makes 4 20-22 cm pasties
500 g bread flour
1/2 teaspoon salt
60 g lard
60 g hard margarine
180 ml approx. water
200 g sliced onion
200 g sliced swede or turnip
400 g finely chopped chuck steak or skirt
600 g sliced potatoes
salt and pepper

Rub half of the lard into flour sifted with salt. Cube the rest of the fats and mix roughly with the flour. Add the water and knead to a smooth stetchable dough. Rest, divide into four and roll out to form four 22 cm circles. Preheat the oven to 220 C, gas mark 7. Sprinkle onion and swede across the middle of each pasty. Season. lay meat on top. Spread some potato on the meat and season. Cover with more potatoes (According to Hettie Merrick, you shouldn't season the top layer of potato because it makes the pastry taste bitter.)

Brush water round the edges of the paste, but only in a half-moon. Lift the moistened edge to the dry one and seal. Tuck in the corners. Crimp the edges by folding them over in a series of small pleats. Lay the pasties on a baking sheet, brush with milk or egg. Bake 30 minutes and turn down oven to 150 C, gas mark 2. Bake 30 minutes more.

Muggety Pie

The umbilical cords of calves were once used for this popular pie. Chitterlings, the intestines of pigs or veal are still sold by a handful of craft butchers across the South West and make a good alternative. This curiosity from an early W.I. book of Cornish specialities, ancient and modern, describes one way of using them:

"Take the long cord of a calf, clean it, soak it for an hour in salt water then boil a short time. Cut cord lengthways with a pair of scissors. Cut into convenient lengths, place in a pie dish with pepper and salt, and flour to taste. Add onions if liked and a white sauce. Cover with pastry and bake."

Cod Pasty

Cornish cooks think putting fish in pastry is an anathema, though recipes for mackerel pasties do occur and Mousehole's celebrated Stargazey Pie, with pilchards poking out of it, is often cited as a regional delicacy.

Serves 4
300 g flour
salt, pepper
150 g hard margarine
milk
175 g skinned cod fillet
50 g butter
50 g diced onion
1 small grated carrot
50 g diced green streaky bacon
115 g diced potato
50 g smoked cod's roe (optional)
1 tablespoon tomato ketchup
1 egg

Sift the flour with a pinch of salt. Rub the margarine into the flour and add enough milk to make a smooth dough. Work into a ball and divide into four. Roll out the pastry and cut out 4 x 18 cm circles. Chop the cod coarsely. Heat butter in a pan and sweat the onion, carrot, bacon and potato over a low heat. Once the potato is almost cooked, stir in the cod, cod's roe and ketchup off the heat. Check seasoning and cool.

Spoon filling on to the circles of pastry. Brush water over the edges and crimp the pasties. Make a small slit in the top of each one, brush with beaten egg and bake 35 minutes in preheated oven, 190 C, gas mark 5

Herby Pie

Beet leaves, spinach, swiss chard, parsley, chives, borage, lettuce hearts, cresses, leek, potato tops (though they're poisonous), blackcurrant leaves and wild orange all figure in versions of this typical baked, batter pudding. It's a dish for hard times and when there was a little in the larder; cooks would add a rasher or two of bacon.

Serves 6
250 g spinach leaves
100 g diced leeks
1 cupful roughly chopped broadleaf parsley
1/2 cupful watercress tops
Herbs to taste: lovage, sorrel, chives or tarragon
salt and pepper
50 g butter
2 eggs
150 ml milk
120 g flour

Blanch all the vegetables and herbs in salted water, just long enough for them to wilt. Drain, press out excess moisture, season and put them in

a buttered baking tin (25 cm x 15 cm approx). Preheat oven to 220 C, gas mark 7. Whisk eggs, milk. salt and pepper 5 minutes. Fold flour into the milk. Pour mixture over the herbs and bake till crisp and risen, roughly 20 minutes.

Saffron Cake

There are more than ten versions of this genuine regional speciality. That's a testimony to its popularity, but shows how freely individual cooks interpreted it. Saffron disappeared from the duchy about 1900, but it was never widely grown except in the North-East. The best comes from La Mancha in Spain, but because of its price Cornish bakeries substitute anatto, a coloured vegetable dye. This completely devalues the recipe turning it into no more than a tea bread or bun.

Makes 1 large loaf
15 g fresh yeast
2 tablespoons tepid water
2 x .125 g sachets Manchegan saffron
500 g bread flour
1 tablespoon salt
2 tablespoon sugar
200 g mixed currants, rasins and sultanas
grated nutmeg
5 eggs
250 g softened butter

Crumble the yeast and dissolve it in water. Sprinkle saffron over it. Sift flour, salt, sugar and nutmeg. Mix the yeast and 3 beaten eggs together. Add to the flour and knead, preferably with an electric mixer (dough hook attachment). Add the remaining eggs one at a time, then the dried fruit. Continue to knead till elastic, about 15 minutes. Incorporate the butter a few knobs at a time. The dough becomes sticky then supple and shiny. Cover with a cloth and leave to double its volume in a warm place. Knock it back and mould it on a floured surface. Put into a greased cake or bread tin and leave it to rise again. Preheat the oven to 200 C, gas mark 6. Bake 50 minutes (cover the top with foil, if it colours too quickly. Leave to stand 5 minutes and turn on to a cooling wire.

Note: old recipes flavoured this cake with cinnamon, cloves, mace and caraway seeds

---

Heavy Cake

'Fuggan' is described in a Cornish dictionary as 'a cake made of flour and raisins, often eaten by miners for dinner.' It was contrasted with the hoggan, a similar formula baked with a slice of pork or bacon on top. There are many recipes for heavy cake, but they all approximate to 3 parts flour, 2 parts fat (or clotted cream) and one part sugar. They may contain dried fruit. They are always decorated with criss-cross cuts across the top.

Serves 8
300 g strong flour
pinch of salt
100 g currants
100 g light, soft brown sugar
200 g butter
a little milk

Combine the flour salt, currants and sugar. Roughly mix in the butter. Add a little milk and knead to form a ball. Roll out the pastry into a rectangle. Fold the two ends of the long side into the middle and fold in half so you have four layers. Rest 20 minutes. Roll out again and repeat the folding. Roll and fold a third time. The cake will be about 4 cm thick. Preheat the oven to 190 C, gas mark 5. Mark the cake with criss-cross cuts like a fishing net's mesh. Put it on a baking sheet and bake 45 minutes approx.

Note: an early recipe describes the texture as 'light and shaley'. Another interesting way of creating this effect is to roll it out, roll it up, roll it out again in the opposite direction to which it has been rolled up and finally roll it up again.

Apple and Date Dickie

When the NFU sent out a call for regional recipes in 1996, it received this one from Esme Francis, living in St Just, titled Granny Routleff's Cornish Recipe.

Serves 8–10
450 g flour
110 g pastry lard
water
450 g sliced apple
110 g dates
sugar
milk

Sift the flour, rub in the fat. Add a little water, work into a ball and roll out. Halve the pastry and roll out pieces to fit an oblong baking tin. Preheat the oven to 190 C, gas mark 5. Line the tin with one sheet of pastry. Cover it with the apple, dates and sugar, then the second layer of pastry. Brush the top with a little milk and sugar to glaze. 'Bake for half-an-hour or so.'

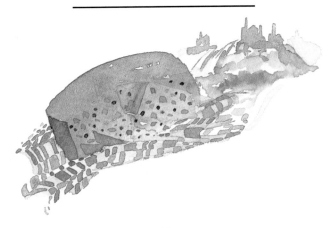

Cornish Black Cake

Cornish cooks past seem to have enjoyed an insatiable appetite for currants. They crop up in the biscuits called 'Squashed Flies', a kind of Spotted Dick known in dialect as 'Currany 'Obbin', in Pitchy Cake, similar to fruit bread, Sly Cakes made from rolled up flaky pastry and their own version of a rich fruit cake.

Makes 1 x 20 cm cake
400 g currants
400 g other mixed dried fruit
220 g softened butter
220 g dark brown sugar
4 eggs
140 g flour sifted with 140 g rice flour
2 teaspoons mixed spice
1 tablespoon black treacle
200 ml brandy
100 g fresh breadcrumbs

Line the cake tin with baking parchment. It should cover the bottom and stand about 2 cm above the top of the sides. Preheat the oven to 170 C, gas mark 3. Combine dried fruit. Cream butter and sugar. Beat in the eggs one at a time alternating each egg with a spoonful of flour to prevent curdling. Fold in the rest of the flour. Add the spice, brandy, treacle, breadcrumbs and finally the fruit. Spoon the mixture into the lined tin, leaving a well in the centre. Bake 2 $^{1}/_{2}$ hours and turn out.

Devon

'Devon pot cakes, pilchard and leek pie, Devon dumplings, drip-ping cakes, chicken and parsley pie, beef and egg pie, Salcombe squab pie.'

These lost dishes were listed in **Where Shall We Eat** *(1936)*
by Florence White founder of the English Folk Cookery Society.
Hers was the first attempt to record the folk recipes of
England. She was especially strong on Devonshire where
she had worked as a girl.

Dartmouth Pie

The South West, and Devon in particular, has many old recipes for mutton pie. Most are very simple, some are quite curious. For instance, one version calls for half a pound of parsley including the roots in its ingredients. They taste like celeriac, but are mildly toxic.

Dartmouth Pie evolved from the years when Tom Jaine, later to be editor of the *Good Food Guide*, was working with Joyce Molyneux at the Carved Angel. They took the idea from Cassell's Dictionary of Food, a rival to Mrs Beeton's Book of Household Management, and spiced it up with apricots and prunes.

Serves 6
900 g mutton
salt
spices: 2 level tsps black peppercorns, 1 blade mace, 1 level tsp allspice berries, 2 tsps coriander seeds
dripping
450 g sliced onions
1 tbsp flour
450 ml beef or lamb stock
150 g dried apricots
150 g pitted prunes
100 g raisins
juice and grated zest of an orange (preferably Seville)

225 g shortcrust pasty
1 beaten egg

Cut the meat into large cubes and salt. Grind the spices to a powder in a spice or coffee mill. Brown the meat in hot dripping and sprinkle on spices. Saute one minute more and add flour and onion. Mix well and pour in the stock. Put the fruit including orange into a large saucepan, add the fried meat and onions. Cover with a tight-fitting lid and bake in a low 150 C, gas mark 2 oven for 1 ½ to 2 hours.

Put a pie funnel in the middle of a large pie dish and pack the meat and fruit around it. Roll out the pastry to 4 mm thick, cut an extra strip long enough to go round the pie dish. Brush dish with water and fix the pastry band to it. Brush band with water. Cover the pie dish with rest of the pastry. Brush with egg and decorate with trimmings. Bake 30 minutes at 200 C, gas mark 6, then turn down heat to 180 C, gas mark 4 and bake for 20 minutes more.

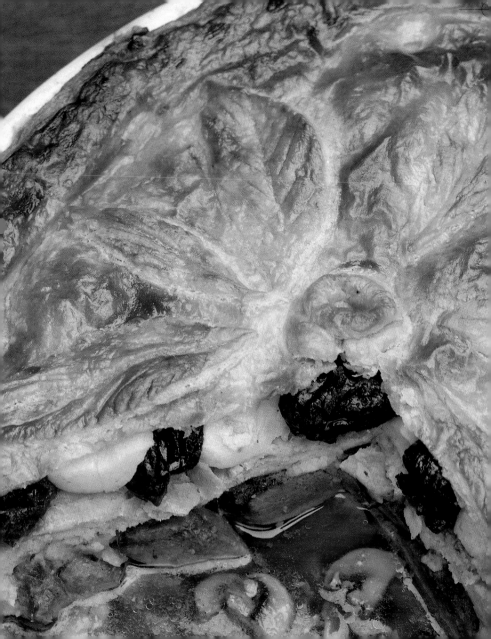

Squab Pie

Squabs are specially reared young pigeons, but as long ago as the 18th century, the name was hi-jacked to cover dishes containing lamb or mutton or even pork. *British Cookery*, a compendium of traditional recipes, published in the 1970s jumped both ways by giving a hybrid version with both pigeon and mutton in it. This, however, is an adaptation of a double-crusted pigeon pie discovered by the great apologist of British cooking, Michael Smith.

Serves 8
1 crushed garlic clove
350 g leg of lamb, sliced finely
4 derinded slices of streaky bacon
400 g chopped field mushrooms
3 cloves
500 ml stock made from their legs and carcasses
12 pigeon breasts
suet paste: 150 g SR flour, 70 g suet, water, salt
4 apples, preferably Devonshire Quarrenden
12 cooked and stoned prunes
250 g puff pastry, beaten egg.
salt and pepper

Sprinkle garlic over the bottom of a large pie dish. Quickly fry the bacon and line the bottom of the dish. Fry the mushrooms in the same pan and put them with the bacon. Lay seasoned lamb slices on top plus the cloves. Next lay the pigeon breasts on these. Pour over half the stock. Season. Make a soft dough with flour, suet, water and a pinch of salt. Roll it out and lay it like a duvet on the pigeons. Bake 90 minutes at 180 C, gas mark 4.

Take the pie from the oven and pour the rest of the stock over the crust. Peel, quarter and core the apples. Lay them with the prunes on the crust. Season. Cover with rolled out flaky pastry. Brush egg wash over it. Bake 40 minutes in a hot oven, 200 C, gas mark 6.

Devon Cut Rounds

The most famous commercial Devon biscuit, the Half Moon, was created in 1826 by Bowden & Co of South Molton and is still being baked professionally in the town - it's like a rusk.

Cut Rounds, popular in Exeter and Barnstaple and simple to make, are more homespun, an alternative to scones or a good accompaniment for many of the new cheeses which are being made throughout the South West. They can be made either with yeast or baking powder to achieve a short and crumbly texture or be quite chewy as here.

Makes 12-15
450 g flour
2 tsps baking powder
1 tsp caster sugar

1 tsp salt
200 ml approx. tepid unskimmed milk

Sift the dry ingredients twice. Add the milk, mix in and knead to form a smooth, dryish dough. Rest 30 minutes. Roll out to 2 cm thickness, Cut out 6 cm circles. Line a baking sheet with silicone paper. Put the circles on the sheet and rest 30 minutes in a warm dry place. Bake roughly 12 minutes in a hot oven 200 C, gas mark 6.

The county boasts two other sweet biscuits.

Devon Flats:
500 g flour, 250 ml clotted cream, 250 g sugar, 1 egg and enough milk to make a smooth, stiffish dough.
Roll out fine, cut out 5 cm circles and bake in a hot oven.

Devonshire Biscuits:
500 g flour, 250 g butter, 250 g sugar, 60 g ground almonds, 4 egg yolks, milk to bind.
Roll out to 6 mm thick, cut out 6 cm circles and bake about 15 minutes at 180 C, gas mark 4.

Shaun Hill's
Chocolate Fudge Cake

Gidleigh Park is a half-timbered Tudoresque mansion, built between the wars by an Aussie shipping magnate. On the fringe of Dartmoor, it's backed by ancient woodland and a branch of the River Teign gurgles over stones beside an immaculate croquet lawn. Until 1994, the chef at this immaculate hotel was Shaun Hill. For balmy summer teas on the terrace he would serve this rich, sticky chocolate cake.

Serves 10-12
225 g unsalted butter
380 g caster sugar
6 eggs
220 g dark chocolate
vanilla essence
110 g ground almonds
150 g fresh white breadcrumbs
For icing:
80 g cocoa powder
250 g sifted icing sugar
110 g unsalted butter

Cream the butter and sugar. Beat in the eggs two at a time. Melt the chocolate over a bowl of simmering water and combine with the egg mixture. Add the vanilla, then fold in the ground almonds and the breadcrumbs. Line a 25 cm baking tin with baking parchment. Preheat the oven to 160 C, gas mark 3. Pour the mixture into the tin and bake 1 hour, or until baked. Turn on to a cooling wire.

Beat cocoa powder, icing sugar and melted butter till smooth. Spread over the cake and leave at least 30 minutes to set.

Apple Dappy

Heather Knee converted the family farm in Topsham, where she was brought up, into the Georgian Tea Rooms. This is her mother's recipe.

Serves 4-6
Butter to grease the dish
300 g SR flour
120 g pastry margarine
60 ml milk (approx.)
400 g peeled, cored and diced cooking apples
100 g demerara sugar
1 teaspoon mixed spice
2 tablespoons golden syrup

Preheat the oven to 160 C, gas mark 3. Butter an ovenproof dish (roughly 25 cm x 20 cm). Crumb the flour and fat, add the milk and knead lightly to form a smooth dough. Roll out to form a rectangle. Sprinkle apple over the top of it. Add sugar and spice. Roll up like a swiss roll. Cut into 2 cm slices. Arrange side by side in the buttered dish. Brush with warm syrup mixed with a tablespoon of water. Bake 30 -35 minutes. Accompany with cream or custard.

Note: blackberries, blackcurrants or other soft fruit mixed with the apple make an appetizing variation.

Railway Cakes

The Barnstaple Book of Cookery (1914) provides a rare insight into what was being served in North Devon at the outbreak of The Great War. It was sponsored by the local gentry, Countess Fortescue, Lady Rosamond Christie, the Mayor and Mayoress of Barnstaple, but it is also a fascinating compilation of culinary jottings by ordinary housewives living in the town.

Few are truly Devonian but they illustrate the extent to which cooking played an integral part in social and cultural life. Mrs Andrews, living at 2 Ebberly Lawn supplied the following, an early, but effective version of the all-in-one cake recipe!

'1 teacupful of flour, 1 teacupful castor sugar, 2 teaspoonsful of baking powder, 2 ozs butter, 2 eggs, a pinch of salt.
Method –Thoroughly mix together and bake in small patty-pans for about 10 minutes.'

The same book also describes a Railway Pudding whose ingredients sound rather less appetizing: the weight of one egg in fat, and two in sugar and flour – the start of the decline in railway catering!

Delicious Little Fluffy Cakes

Here is another gem from *The Barnstaple Book of Cookery* (1914).

Makes 12
170 g softened unsalted butter
120 g castor sugar
2 eggs
220 g cornflour
1 tsp baking powder
1 tablespoon milk
vanilla essence
ground rice

Preheat the oven to 220 C, gas mark 7. Cream the butter and sugar. Beat in the eggs one at a time. Sift flour and baking powder twice. Fold into the creamed base. Thin out to a dropping texture with milk flavoured with vanilla. Grease a tray of patty pans and sprinkle rice over them. Half fill them with mixture and bake for about 12 minutes.

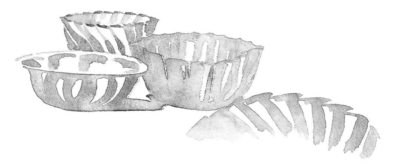

Dorset

A Lark Pie

'Take as many larks as you please, season them with pepper and salt, put some forcemeat in their bellies and balls of the same in the pie with them, lay some very thin slices of bacon upon the larks if you like it, if not put some butter, put in a little thin gravy when it comes out of the oven give it a shake; to have a fine lark pie add a few palates – lambs stones or sweetbreads, hard yolks of eggs, asparagus tops, dryd mushrooms; make a ragoo of all these things and when the larks are bak'd open the pie and throw it over the larks, give it a shake and let it stand $^1/_4$ of an hour by the fire.'

From an early recipe manuscript, published in
Dorset Dishes of the 17th Century, edited by J. Stevens Cox

Portland Dough Cake

This very rich old English dough cake (a kind of yeasted fruit bread) appeared in *What's Cooking in Dorset*, an early W.I. publication. It belongs to the same family as German stollen and Italian panettone. I've adapted it slightly here.

Serves 6–8
400 g bread flour
1/2 teaspoon salt
1 teaspoon dried yeast
or 12 g fresh yeast
150 ml tepid water
70 g dark soft brown sugar
pinch of mixed spice
120 g currants
150 butter or lard

Mix flour and salt. Dissolve yeast in water. Add it to 250 g flour and knead to form a smooth elastic dough. Cover and leave to double its size in a warm place. Knock back and incorporate, sugar, spice, currants, fat and remaining flour. Mould into a large ball or sausage shape. Put on a baking tray, cover and prove again (2–3 hours in a warm place). Preheat the oven to 200 C, gas mark 6. Bake 50 minutes. Cover with foil if it browns too quickly. Turn onto a cooling wire and brush with melted butter.

Dorset Apple Cake

What differentiates Dorset's apple cake from those of other counties is that its two halves are sandwiched together. It's a cake for eating at once, not keeping because it will quickly dry out.

Serves 6–8
250 g SR flour
pinch of salt
200 g unsalted butter
120 g caster sugar
500 g chopped cooking apples
2 beaten eggs
50 g currants
grated zest of lemon
40 g demerara sugar

Preheat the oven to 200 C, gas mark 6. Mix flour and salt and rub in 150 g butter till crumbly. Add the apples, eggs and lemon to make a stiff dough. Empty into two Victoria sandwich tins. Bake about 35 minutes. turn out onto a cooling wire. Sandwich the two halves together with half the remaining butter. Brush top with the rest of the butter and sprinkle demerara on top.

Blueberry Pot Cake

Blueberries are a relatively new addition to Dorset's agricultural heritage. They were introduced by James Trehane in 1949 and his son Jeremy has carried on the family business. Pot cake is much older. Made small they are forerunners of American muffins.

Serves 6
350 g SR flour
grated zest of 1/2 lemon
170 g softened butter
90 g caster sugar
1 beaten egg
170 ml unskimmed milk
220 g blueberries

Preheat the oven to 150 C, gas mark 2. Mix flour and zest, rub in the butter and add the sugar. Combine egg and milk and add it to the flour base to obtain a dropping consistency. Fold in the blueberries. Empty the mixture into a greased, ceramic flower-pot lined with baking parchment, taking care to stop the hole in the bottom. Bake for about 90 minutes till done (time depends on shape and type of container). Our forebears used to split open the warm cake and spread softened butter mixed with demerara sugar on it.

Easter Biscuits

Makes 12
60 g softened butter
110 g sugar
2 egg yolks
250 g flour
1/2 teaspoon ginger
40 g currants

Cream butter and sugar. Beat in the egg. Incorporate the flour sifted with ginger and finally the currants. Roll out on a lightly floured surface. Prick all over. Cut out circles. Put on a greased baking tray, pricked side down. Chill 30 minutes. Preheat oven to 180 C, gas mark 4 and bake 15-20 minutes.
Brush immediately with extra melted lard or butter.

Cranbourne Bisketts

'Rub an ounce of butter into a pound of flour, put the yolk of an egg, a spoonful of yeast into as much warm milk as will mix the flour. Let it lye to rise an hour cut it out without rolling it, and let it lye by the fire till put in the oven. Reserve a little milk and yolk of egg to do over the bisketts with a feather.
They are very good if cut long.'

Were these a rival to or a precursor of the Dorset Knob, still baked by S. Moores of Morcombelake? The word biscuit itself means twice-cooked and these would probably turn out like rolls unless they were dried out in a slow oven after the initial baking. The clue as to what they were like comes in the last sentence's 'cut long'. I think that these may have been a West Country version of grissini.

Makes 36
7 g dried yeast
250 ml tepid milk
30 g butter
1 egg yolk
450 g flour with a pinch of salt
egg and milk to glaze

Dissolve yeast in milk. Rub butter and yolk into the flour. Add the liquid and knead to a smooth dough. Cover and leave to rise in a warm place. Cut into pieces weighing about 20 g each. Either flatten them with the palm of the hand and work them into a ball or roll them out into long sticks as though they were plasticine. Put them on baking sheets. Leave to rise about 30 minutes. Preheat the oven to 220 C, gas mark 8. Brush with egg and milk and bake 15 minutes. Remove from the oven and cool. Put the oven at lowest setting. Reintroduce the biscuits and dry out for at least an hour till crisp.

Gloucestershire

'Such a pie was the Gloucester Royal Pie, part of the city's tribute to the throne from the time of Richard III to Queen Victoria. It was made of lampreys caught in the Severn, crayfish and truffles, with many other ingredients, all set in aspic jelly. The crust was decorated with crayfish set on golden skewers and with a gold crown and sceptre Four golden lions supported the dish, and there was a banner with the arms of Gloucester.'

Elisabeth Ayrton, *The Cookery of England*

Lemon Pies

One of the signature dishes of the Roux Brothers is a tarte au citron.
Its lemon filling is almost identical to a recipe described as 'ancestral'
from the Gloucestershire Women's Institute:

> *'The yellow rind of 1 large lemon pounded with 4 oz fine white sugar.*
> *Add the yolks of 3 eggs and half the whites whisked to snow.*
> *Continue whisking while adding ¹/₂ lb just melted butter (or half clotted*
> *cream), the juice of lemon being beaten in last with a few spots of*
> *orange flower brandy. Line patty pans with very fine puff paste.*
> *Fill with the lemon mixture and bake.'*

This is how to make it as a single pie for 6

250 g good shortcrust pastry

4 large eggs

grated zest and juice of 1 lemon

100 g caster sugar

250 ml double cream

2 teaspoons Grand Marnier

Line a greased 20 cm tart ring with the pastry. Rest 30 minutes.
Preheat the oven to 200 C, gas mark 6. Line the inside of the pastry
case with baking parchment and fill with baking beans. Bake blind 15
minutes. Separate the yolks from the whites. Take the tart from the
oven and remove the beans. Brush the inside of the pastry with a little
egg white. Return to the oven for five minutes and turn down
temperature to 150 C, gas mark 2. Whisk the yolks, one white, lemon

zest and sugar till thick and creamy. Beat in the cream, followed by the lemon juice and Grand Marnier. Pour into the pastry shell and bake 40 – 45 minutes until golden and set.

Whit Pot

In A Taste Of The West Country, Theodora Fitzgibbon, identified White Pot with Gloucestershire, claiming it was served at revels and feasts through the year, but the dish is properly Whit Pot, linking it to Whitsun and its fame stretched across the border to Somerset. The earliest recipe goes back to *The Closet of the Eminently Learned Sir Kenelm Digbie Kt* (1669) when the dish was like bread pudding.

Serves 4
butter
2 heaped tablespoons flour
2 tablespoons milk
500 ml boiled single cream
2 heaped tablespoons golden syrup or corn syrup
nutmeg

Butter a pint and a half pie dish. Preheat the oven to 170 C, gas mark 3. Mix the flour with milk in a bowl. Beat in cream gradually and stir in syrup. Pour mixture into the pie dish and grate nutmeg over it. Bake, like rice pudding for about 90 minutes till set, with a golden brown skin on top. Serve cold with bottled fruit, such as damsons or plums.

Clifton Puffs

Clifton was once on the main stagecoach route from Banbury and Cheltenhan into Bristol. The little pastries which take their name from the town (now part of the city) have much in common with Banbury cakes in that they are made from a flaky pastry enclosing a mincemeat-like filling.

Makes about 16
270 g butter
250 g bread flour
pinch of salt
1 tablespoon lemon juice
60 ml approx. iced water
70 g ground almonds
120 g grated apple
120 g currants
60 g seeded raisins
60 g chopped peel
170 g chopped almonds
grated nutmeg
4 tablespoons cider brandy
egg and demerara sugar for glaze

Rub 70 g of butter into flour, sifted with salt. Add the water mixed with lemon juice and work into a smooth dough. Sprinkle almonds on the work surface and roll the pastry out in a rectangular shape.

Dot the rest of the butter over two-thirds of the rectangle. Fold the uncovered pastry over the butter and over again to encase it. Seal the edges. Roll out to form a rectangle again, as thin as possible without the butter breaking through the pastry. Fold the two ends in towards the middle and fold them again together as though you were closing a book. Seal edges and rest 15 minutes. Roll out again and repeat the folding process. Rest and repeat once more. Rest and roll out the pastry as fine as you can. Divide into 12 cm squares. Preheat the oven to 220 C, gas mark 7.

Mix the other ingredients except for the glaze together. Pile little mounds in the middle of each square. Fold corner to corner and seal edges. Brush with egg and sprinkle with sugar. Put on a watered baking sheet and bake about 15 minutes.

Upside Down Greengage Cake

Upside-down cakes are the English answer to the French Tarte Tatin. In early recipes a cake tin was lined with pineapple slices, sponge mixture was poured on top and baked. In the version of David Everitt-Matthias, owner of the Champignon Sauvage in Cheltenham, the base is a rich concoction of almonds and the greengages are caramelized.

16 greengages
80 g butter
210 g caster sugar
1 vanilla pod

grated zest and juice of 1/2 orange
1 vanilla pod
70 g flour
1/2 tsp baking powder
pinch of salt
100 g milk
40 g ground almonds
1 beaten egg

Stone and quarter the greengages. Melt 30 g butter and 150 g of sugar in a pan. Boil till golden. Add the greengages and cook about 3 minutes to an amber caramel and set aside. Preheat the oven to 230 C, gas mark 8. Arrange the greengages and some of their caramel in four 7–8 cm tartlet tins. Cream the rest of the butter and caster sugar.
Add grated zest and, the scraped vanilla seeds. Mix in flour, baking powder, salt, then the orange juice, milk, almonds and egg. Spoon over the greengages. Bake 15 minutes. Cool 5 minutes and turn out.

A sorbet to accompany the cake:
**500 ml water, 300 g granulated sugar, 100 g glucose
750 g liquidized greengages**

Bring the water, sugar and glucose to the boil, stirring to dissolve the sugar. Cool. Mix 500 ml of the syrup with the fruit. Put it into the ice cream machine and churn till frozen.
David Everitt-Matthias spoons raisins soaked in rum over the sorbet as a garnish.

Somerset

Until the turn of the century many Somerset homes had no ovens and families used public bakehouses where they paid a small charge. The following story from the South Somerset Herald describes what happened when a couple discovered that the manageress was stealing some of their baked potatoes.

'It was decided that when the husband fetched the dinner on the next occasion he would gently broach the complaint to the lady who presided over the bakehouse. He did so. The lady was warm as a result of her exertions and repudiated his insinuations in a very forcible manner. The poor man felt stung with her tongue, his ire was aroused with the result that he came away in a towering rage. On reaching home he opened the door of the cottage, threw the dinner in the middle of the floor and told his wife that in future she would have to face the mistress of the house for he would no more do with it. He promptly went off to his favourite public house and drowned his sorrow in beer.'

Priddy Oggies

'How old does a dish have to be before it can be reckoned 'regional'?' asked Jane Grigson in her *Observer Guide To British Cookery*. She was referring to the Priddy Oggy, invented at the Miner's Arms, Priddy by Paul Leyton in 1968. Oggy is slang for pasty in Cornwall, and since Priddy was a mining village long before it became famous for its snails, the borrowing seems appropriate.

Serves 8
30 g butter
30 g pastry shortening
200 g mature Cheddar, grated
100 ml water
250 g flour
pinch of salt
2 pork tenderloins (600 g approx.)
chopped parsley (or rosemary)
salt and tabasco
beaten egg
8 slices Denhay ham

Cream the fats in a bowl, add 100 g cheese and water. Sift flour and salt and crumb flour and fats. Divide into four roughly kneaded cakes. Roll out to 1 cm thick, brush with water and stick them together in 4 layers. Divide into 4 and repeat the process. Rest the dough and do it once again. Cut this flaky pastry into eight and roll out in 8 x 15 cm circles.

Split the pork fillets lengthways without quite cutting through them. Flatten with a cutlet bat or rolling pin so that the meat forms two rectangles, roughly 1-2 centimetre thick. Spread the remaining cheese, parsley, salt and tabasco over the meat. Roll up the meat to envelope the cheese and put into a freezer for 45 minutes to firm up. Cut each piece into four and wrap each one in the ham. Lay a piece of meat in the middle of a pastry circle, brush its edges with water, fold together and crimp the edges.

Brush with egg and make a hole for the steam to escape. Bake 30 minutes in a preheated oven, 190 C, gas mark 5, for 20 - 25 minutes.

Note: in the earliest recipe, the 'oggy' was started off in a low oven and then transferred to a deep frier to finish cooking.

Bath Olivers

Dr William Oliver, born in Penzance in 1695, went to Bath in 1734 to see whether the city's famous mineral water was all it had been pumped up to be. He stayed there for the rest of his life. While he was living there he set up his coachman, Atkins, as a baker at No 13 Green Street, providing him with £100 and ten sacks of flour and he also supplied his own recipe for thin, brittle biscuits which he had been dishing out to patients suffering from dyspepsia. The biscuits became an instant fashionable success and are still baked today. Originally, they were hand cut, sandwiched in pairs and pricked over to prevent blistering, but now they are manufactured and bear the image of their creator embossed upon them.

Bath Biscuits

Apart from its buns and Bath Olivers, the city has another, lesser known biscuit. This recipe appeared, in manuscript form, in the pocket book of the 19th century Edinburgh baker, John Colville of Portobello. He actually used a higher proportion of flour, than is given in this more recent version.

Makes about 30
125 g unsalted butter
140 g caster sugar
2 medium eggs (125 g by weight)
180 g soft cake flour
1/2 teaspoon baking powder
mixed spice
optional: grated lemon zest

Preheat the oven to 190 C, gas mark 5. Cover a baking sheet with parchment. Cream the butter and sugar. Beat in the egg a little at a time. Sift the flour, baking powder and spice, mixing in the lemon zest if you use it. Incorporate the flour into the creamed mix. Fill a piping, bag fitted with a plain tube. Pipe fingers onto the parchment, chill 30 minutes and bake for about 12 minutes till done.

Note: If you prefer biscuits very crisp, cool them and give them a second bake for 15 minutes in a low oven (150 C).

Sally Lunns

Sally Lunns, or Spring Garden Cakes as they were known at one time during their 300 year history, are a Bath institution. There are three legends as to their origin. In version one, Sally Louan, a Huguenot refugee, started making a kind of brioche for a Bath baker about 1680. The second pretender is supposed to have hawked her cakes around the city in Beau Nash's day.

The third possibility is that the name is a corruption of Soleil Lune, a fanciful French description of the golden, round topped bun. The Bath Chronicle of 1796 carried a recipe in verse which began:

> *No more I heed the muffin's zest,*
> *The yeast cake or the bun.*
> *Sweet muse of pastry teach me how*
> *To make a Sally Lunn.*

Home-made Sally Lunns aren't as good as those baked in the eponymous teashop in Lilliput Alley, behind Bath Abbey. They look like a light, fluffy teabread. The only criticism of them is that they are sold with baked beans, goat's cheese, egg mayonnaise and other incongruous sweet and savoury toppings. Traditionally, they should be split open warm like a scone and liberally spread with clotted cream. They are excellent toasted with butter and cinnamon.

A scrummy filling adapted from Silvija Davidson's recipe in *Loaf, Crust and Crumb*: Toast four slices of Sally Lunn, spread with lemon curd, clotted cream on top, serve with either stewed blackberries or loganberries poached with sugar and cinnamon.

Cider Cake

Cider cake was popular throughout the South West and up into Hereford, Worcester and Oxford, but Florence White, the pioneering historian of regional food in the 1930s links it to Bath, probably because it was once well-known for its walnut trees. Early cookery writers claimed that guinea fowl eggs were better for baking and they are very rich, but the important thing is size. Like bantam eggs they are small and the yolk to white ratio seems higher. This recipe is adapted from Elizabeth Ayrton's *English Provincial Cooking*.

Serves 8
120 g unsalted butter
120 g caster sugar
3 bantam or other small eggs
240 g SR flour
60 g chopped walnuts
grated nutmeg
up to 150 ml sweet farmhouse cider

Preheat the oven to 190 C. Line a 20 cm baking tin. Cream the butter and sugar. Beat in the eggs a little at a time. Fold in the flour, nuts and grate in the nutmeg. Lighten with as much of the cider as the mixture will take to form a thickish dropping consistency. Pour in the tin and bake 50 to 60 minutes. Leave five minutes to cool in the tin and turn out. This can also be served as a pudding with a berry sauce and clotted cream.

Whortleberry Pie

Throughout the rest of England, whortleberries are called bilberries and the great food historian, Dorothy Hartley described tarts made from them as 'the best on earth!' Beacause the berries throw out a lot of juice and lose volume when cooked, they were often baked with roasted apples (an alternative to blackberry and apple pie).

Double crusted pies are better baked in ovens with a hot floor.

Serves 6
butter
250 g flour
130 g pastry shortening
55 ml milk
2 tablespoons rice flour
350 g whortleberries
juice 1/2 lemon
130 g sugar
milk and sugar for glazing

Butter a 22 cm pie plate. Crumb the flour and the fat. Add the milk and work into a smooth ball. Cut the pastry into two. Roll out one piece, prick it and line the plate. Sprinkle half rice flour over it. Pile the whortleberries mixed with lemon juice, sugar and remaining rice flour on top, leaving room to seal the edges. Moisten these. Roll out the rest of the paste for the lid. Fit it and crimp the edges. Rest 20 minutes. Preheat the oven to 220 C, gas mark 7. Brush the top of the pie with milk and dust with sugar. Bake 10 minutes, reduce heat to 180 C., gas mark 4 and bake 25 minutes more. Eat cold.

At the Castle Hotel, Taunton there is a tradition, going back 60 years, of serving Whortleberry Pie to the visiting Australian cricket team.

Sir Donald Bradman, taken ill during a tour match with the county, was revived by a pie at the Castle where the team was staying. Over the years, the recipe has evolved and become more like an open flan. To make it the current chef, Phil Vickery, lines a large tart base with a shortbread pastry, bakes it, cools it, covers it with a layer of pastry cream, tops it with stewed 'whorts' and covers them with the juice thickened with arrowroot.

Somerset Raisin Glory

This recipe appeared in a Somerset newspaper's Notes and Queries section during the 1920s. It's a curious blend of flavours and textures, old fashioned, but good nonetheless.

Serves 6-8
350 g rich shortcrust pastry
200 g seeded raisins
110 g grated cheddar (medium farmhouse)
rind and juice of 1/2 lemon
60 g ground almonds
2 drops almond essence
mixed spice
1 beaten egg

Preheat the oven to 190 C, gas mark 5. Line a greased baking tin (22 cm x 18 cm approx.) with half the pastry. Pour boiling water over the raisins. Steep five minutes and drain. Combine them with the other ingredients, bar the egg. Spread the mixture over the pastry. Roll out the rest of the pastry and cover. Brush the top with beaten egg. Score the top with a chequer pattern. Bake about 30 minutes.

Rich shortcrust pastry: Rub 400 g good salted butter into 700 g flour. Work four beaten eggs into the flour and fat so that the paste forms a smooth, silky ball. A beater on a mixing machine is as good as, if not better than fingers – enough for 2-3 tarts but it will freeze

St Catherine Cake

St Catherine is the patron saint of lace makers, so a cake in her honour ought to come from the lace capital of the West, Honiton. However, this cake shaped like a Catherine Wheel probably originated in Frome.

270 g SR flour
1 teaspoon bicarbonate of soda
3 rounded tablespoons ground almonds
almond essence
1/2 teaspoon mixed spice
220 g caster sugar
220 g unsalted butter
1 egg
50 g sultanas
icing sugar

Preheat the oven to 200 C, gas mark 6. Line a baking sheet with parchment. Sift flour and bi-carb. Combine with almonds and essence, mixed spice and sugar. Melt the butter and work in to form a paste. Add the beaten egg. Pour the boiling water over sultanas, steep five minutes and drain. Mix them into the paste. Divide it into six and leave to cool. Flour a work surface and roll out the pieces of paste by hand so they are like little snakes, roughly 2 centimetres in diameter. Arrange them in a spiral like a Catherine wheel on the baking sheet. Bake 20 minutes or till cooked. Slide the parchment and the cake on to a cooling wire, leave to set and dust with icing sugar before serving.

Wiltshire

To make the Marleborough Cake
'Take eight eggs, yolks and whites, beat and strain them, and put to them a pound of sugar, beaten and sifted; beat it three quarters of an hour together, then put three quarters of a pound of flour well dried, and two ounces of caraway seeds; beat it all together, and bake it in a a quick oven in broad tin pans.'

from the *Compleat Housewife* 1753 by E. Smith.

Wiltshire Plait

Depending on one's view of cooking this is either an English alternative to pâté en croûte or a playful variation on the sausage roll theme. It's good eaten hot or cold, but its quality depends on the quality of the pork, which should have a balance of lean and fat and the choice of a really mature cheddar.

Serves 4
300 g minced belly of pork
60 g diced Bramley apple
60 g mature cheddar
40 g finely diced onion
1 crushed garlic clove
5 tablespoons chopped broadleaf parsley
salt and pepper
1 beaten egg
350 g made puff pastry

Mix the pork, apple, cheese, onion, garlic, parsley, seasoning and half the egg. Roll out the pastry to form a 25 cm square. Form the meat into a loaf and lay it in the centre of the pastry. Cut the pastry on either side of it into diagonal 1 cm strips. Dampen the ends and fold the strips alternately from each side over the meat to create a plaited effect. Seal the ends and glaze with remaining egg. Slide onto a damp baking sheet (it helps the paste to puff). Bake 20 minutes in a preheated 220 C, gas mark 7 oven. Reduce to 180 C, gas mark 4 for a further 20–25 minutes.

Bacon Scones

'These scones make a delicious alternative to bread, served hot from the oven and spread thickly with butter at breakfast or teatime or for lunch accompanied by a freshly mixed green salad.'

Angela Rawson, Nikki Kedge, *Wiltshire Cookery*.

Makes 8 pieces
115 g diced smoked streaky bacon
115 g grated onion
4 diced celery sticks
450 g SR flour
pinch of salt
black pepper
1/2 teaspoon mustard powder
50 g dripping
2 tablespoons chopped parsley
1 small beaten egg
150 ml milk approx.

Half-fry the bacon, add the onion and celery and continue to fry them till softened. Cool. Sift flour, salt, pepper and mustard. Rub in the dripping, add the parsley and bacon-vegetable mixture. Combine the egg and $^3/_4$ of the milk, add to the mixture and work to a smooth dough. Mix in the rest of the milk if it seems too dry. Roll out to form a round, put on floured baking sheet. Mark eight segments. Dust the top with flour. Bake 25 minutes at 200 C, gas mark 6 oven. Serve warm.

Rushall Wholemeal Bread

Rushall Mill, near Pewsey, makes this loaf from its own organic flour.

Makes 2 large loaves
85 g fresh yeast
1 1/2 teaspoons sugar
1 1/2 teaspoons vegetable oil
850 ml water at body temperature (37 C)
1.5 kilos Rushall wholemeal flour
25 g salt

Dissolve the yeast and sugar with the oil and water. Sieve the flour over a large bowl and add back the bran remaining in the sieve. Pour the yeast mixture on to the the flour and knead for at least five minutes. Cover and leave to rise in a warm place. Knock back, divide into two. Shape and put into two greased, 900 g bread tins. leave to rise again. Preheat the oven to 230 C, gas mark 8. Bake about 40 minutes. Turn out on to a wire rack and cool.

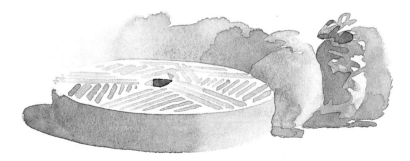

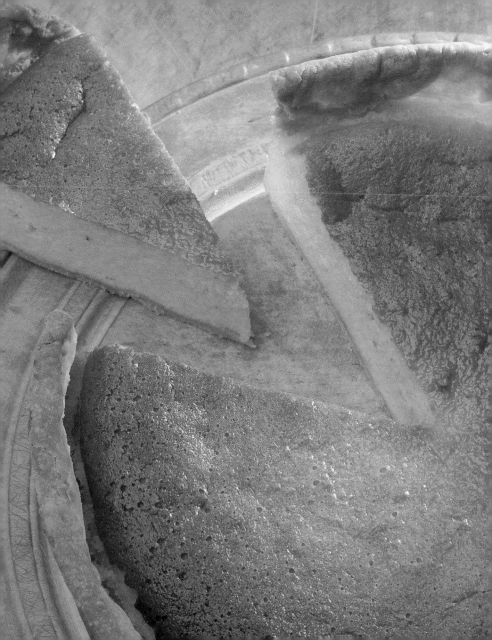

Devizes Cheesecake

The small market town has given its name to two unique recipes a cheesecake and a pie. The latter is extinct – it was a meaty miscellany of calf's head, brains, tongue, sweetbreads and bacon baked under a flour and water paste dough. One version of the cheesecake, made with cake crumbs, is still being baked at Strong's bakery and restaurant in the town. An older version using ground almonds is more luxurious:

'To a pound and a half of cheese curd, put 10 oz of butter, beat both in a mortar until all looks like butter. Then add ¼ pound of almonds, beat fine with orange water, ¾ pound of sugar, 8 eggs half ye whites, a little mace pounded and a little cream. Beat all together a quarter of an hour; bake in puff paste in a quick oven.'

Serves 8-10
250 g puff pastry
275 g curd cheese
170 g unsalted butter
3 eggs + 2 yolks
120 g caster sugar
pinch of ground mace
2 tablespoons orange flower water
120 g ground almonds
splash of almond essence

Roll out the pastry finely, prick the base thoroughly and line a 22 cm flan ring (steep-sided). Rest 30 minutes. Preheat the oven to 200 C, gas mark 6. Line the pastry with baking parchment and fill with baking beans. Bake blind 20 minutes. Remove the beans and parchment. While it's cooking, cream the cheese and butter. Whisk eggs, sugar, mace and orange flower water together. Beat into the the creamed based a little at a time. Alternate with almonds flavoured with essence. Pour into the pastry shell and bake at 170 C, gas mark 3 for 70 minutes.

Boiled Fruit Cake

This traditional method of making fruit cake doesn't require boiling like a pudding, but the fruit and liquid ingredients are cooked together first so that the cake ends up moister and keeps for ages.

Serves 8

Wet ingredients - 150 ml milk plus 100ml brandy

1 tbs golden syrup

rind and juice 1/2 lemon plus 1/2 orange

450 g mixed dried fruit (raisins, currants, sultanas)

150 g chopped almonds

Dry ingredients - 110 g soft brown sugar

150 g grated apple

120 g candied peel

120 g flour mixed with 60 g breadcrumbs

120 g suet

3 teaspoon mixed spice

Boil wet ingredients and leave for 24 hours. Line a 17 cm cake tin with baking parchment. Preheat the oven to 180 C, gas mark 4. Combine dry ingredients with soaked ones and pour in tin. Bake for 65 minutes or till done. Cool 5 minutes and turn out on to a cooling wire.

Lardy Cake

Lard is to Wiltshire what clotted cream is to Devon and Cornwall. The great Elizabeth David suggested that every lardy cake 'oozing with fat, sticky with sugar' should carry a health warning, but added that they were eaten as special treats, not as daily fare.

Makes 10 pieces
30 g dried yeast
320 ml skimmed milk at body temperature, 37 C
500 g bread flour (warmed in a low oven)
35 g caster sugar
1 heaped teaspoon salt
420 g lard
200 g currants
200 g dark soft brown sugar
1 dessert spoon mixed spice
egg wash

Dissolve the yeast in milk. Mix flour, sugar and salt. Rub in 30 g of lard. Add the milk and knead to form a smooth dough. Cover and leave to rise in a warm place till it doubles its volume. Knock back and knead in the currants. Roll into a rectangle roughly 15 cm by 30 cm. Cream the rest of the lard with sugar and spice. Spread it over two-thirds of the rectangle. Fold back the flap of uncovered dough, back over the lard and fold again to encase it (3 dough layers, two lard layers). Press the edges together so the lard doesn't escape. Roll out the dough in the opposite direction to the fold and fold again. Chill 20 minutes and repeat. Chill and repeat once more. Roll out to cover a greased baking sheet. Cover and prove one hour in a warm place. Brush the top with egg wash and mark a trellis pattern with a sharp knife. Preheat the oven to 200 C, gas mark 6 and bake about 40 minutes. Cool before serving.

Baked Hams

The term 'baking' applied to ham has become a misnoma. Once it meant encasing the leg in a thick edible dough, known as huff paste, and cooking it from raw. Done this way the meat effectively boiled, like an egg in its shell. By the middle of the last century, hams were first cooked, usually poached in water, perhaps with the addition of carrots, onions and herbs, till they were almost done. After they were drained, the rind was removed and the fat coated either with a sweet glaze or breadcrumbs before being given a final bake in the oven.

Wiltshire has always been a centre of the ham and bacon industry. The treacle-black Bradenham Ham invented in 1781 is still available from posh grocers. C & T Harris, who produced it (it has had a Royal Warrant since 1888) closed its Calne factory in the 1980s.

Note: Unless you have a pan large enough to take a whole ham, it is more sensible to buy a gammon, once known as Wiltshire ham, because it's cured on the side of pork with the rest of the bacon. It's more manageable.

Before boiling the ham, soak it in several changes of water from one to three days. A gammon needs 24 hours.

Put the meat in the pan, cover it with cold water, heat to 80 C and simmer at this temperature till done. Cooking time will vary according to the shape and weight of the ham. A 6 kilo joint takes about 3 hours. It is more accurate to use a meat or electronic probe and cook until it registers 70 C in the deep muscle next to the bone. Take it from the oven and shave off the rind leaving a layer of fat. Score it with a diamond pattern. Preheat oven to 190 C., gas mark 5, brush the ham with melted glaze (See below) and bake 30 minutes.

Glazes for hams:

**Melt 120 g each soft brown sugar and honey
with 80 ml sweet cider.**

**Dust with 150 g soft brown sugar
and baste during glazing with sweet sherry.**

**Make a paste of 30 g English mustard
30 g dripping or bacon fat
and 140 g honey
and spread over surface.**

Sprinkle breadcrumbs over glaze before baking to obtain a crisp finish.

Suppliers

Pasties, Saffron & Heavy Cakes

The Lizard Pasty Shop
Sunny Corners
The Lizard TR12 7PB
01326 290889

E.Eddy & Son
Jack Lane
Newlyn TR18 5HZ
01736 62535

Martin's Bakery
106 Clifden Road
St Austell PL25 4AP
01726 73681

Ough's
10 Market St
Liskeard PL14 3JJ
01597 343253

Portreath Bakery
3 The Square
Portreath TR16 4LA
01209 842612

Stein's Delicatessen
8 Middle St
Padstow PL28 8AR
01841 532221

W.T.Warren & Son
The Top Shop
Market Square
St Just
Penzance TR19 7HD

Devon
Devon Half Moons

Chanters Bakeries
2 Barnstaple St
South Molton
01769 572651

Cakes

Mrs Gill's Country Cakes
Unit 5
Link House
Leat St
Tiverton EX16 5LG
01884 242744

Breads, Pies
and Pasties

Cottage Bakery
Stoke Fleming
Dartmouth
01803 770259

Portlemouth Pastries
15 Church St
Kingsbridge TQ7 1BS
01548 854073

Treloar's
38 High St
Crediton EX17 3JP

Dorset
Biscuits and Cakes

Fudge's Bakery
Bridge Bakery
Leigh
Sherborne DT9 6HJ
01935 872253

Lower Farmhouse
(Cider Cake)
Sandford Orcas
Sherborne DT9 4RP
01963 220363

S.Moores (Dorset Knobs)
The Biscuit Bakery
Morcombelake
Bridport DT6 6ES
01297 489253

Gloucester
Flour

Shipton Mill
Tetbury GL8 8RP
01666 505050

Bread and Cakes

The Flour Bag
Burford St
Lechlade GL7 3AP
01367 252322

Hobbs House Bakery
39 High St
Chipping Sodbury BS17 6BA
01454 321629

Somerset
Bath Buns

Mountstevens Ltd
Borough Walls
Bath BA1 1QR
01225 460877

Sally Lunns

Sally Lunns
Refreshment House
4 N.Parade Passage
Bath BA1 1NX
01225 461634

Wiltshire
Flour

Rushall Mill
Devizes Road
Rushall
Pewsey SN9 6EB
01980 630335

Acknowledgements

Baking would not have been possible without the help and support of many lovers of the West Country and its cooking, but the real driving force behind this book was the late Florence White whose books on the folk cookery of England, *Where Shall We Eat* (1936) and *Good Things in England* (1932) have been an inspiration.

My special thanks go to Albert Beer, Kit Chapman, David Everitt-Mathias, Esme Francis, Anthony Gibson, Henrietta Green, Geraldene Holt, Tom Jaine, Nikki Kedge, Margaret Kelland, Diane Lethbridge, Joyce Molyneux, Ann Muller, Antoinette Raffael, Angela Rawson, Stephen Ross, George and Amanda Streatfield, Richard Stein and Caroline Yates.

Recipe Index

First published in Great Britain in 1997
Copyright © 1997 Michael Raffael

British Library Cataloguing-in-publication Data
CIP Record for this title is available from the British Library
ISBN 1 874448 11 6

HALSGROVE
Publishing, Media and Distribution
Halsgrove House
Lower Moor Way
Tiverton, Devon EX16 6SS
Tel: 01884 243242 Fax: 01884 243325

Design & Art Direction Andrew Sutterby
Photography Sam Bailey
Illustrations Moish Sokal

Printed in Italy by Tipolitografia Petruzzi Corrado + C.